LIFE
The Year in Pictures

LIFE
The Year in Pictures

INTRODUCTION | Before and After

The first two thirds of the year now seem to have occurred ages ago, and in a way they did. They unfolded in a different time and place, in a bygone era when Americans were, by and large, relaxed, happy and safe.

After a few months in Washington ushering his tax cut through Congress, W took a golfing vacation in Maine. Condit was besieged because there was no one else to besiege. Then, overnight, everything changed. Guardsmen at the airport and the President in his Oval Office meant nothing but business.

This was then: W, Julia's Oscar, sharks, tax cuts, rolling blackouts, Gary Condit, Colin Powell in absentia, Alaska's oil, some kind of drought in Afghanistan. This is now: President Bush, Osama bin Laden, anthrax, Guardsmen at the airport, Colin Powell ascendant, Middle East oil, the taking of Afghanistan, a strange and ongoing war both at home and abroad.

Never have a single day's events caused so abrupt and dramatic a shift in America's focus. Conflict seemed inevitable when the shot heard round the world rang out on Lexington Green in 1775, and war was all but global when the Japanese attacked Pearl Harbor in 1941. But America was so complacently and self-satisfiedly at peace on Sept. 10 that the morning shows could find nothing to bump Condit as a story, while LIFE was starting to

wonder what gravitas might be brought to its annual *Year in Pictures.* Certainly there were international crises that demanded our attention—AIDS as an ever greater plague in Africa, unrest throughout Europe and Asia—but as has often been noted since September 11, the mindset of most Americans had over time shifted from global concerns to at-home matters. Even events that directly impacted U.S. citizens with close ties abroad, such as the continuing strife in Ireland and Israel, were tough sells as front-page news. Above the fold were stories on the latest shark attack. And as you will learn in this book, the much ballyhooed Summer of the Shark wasn't anything extraordinary. The fish filled a vacuum.

Then, suddenly, there was no vacuum, nor would there be one for months, even years to come. As September 11 progressed from morning to afternoon to evening, each of us kept changing our

assessment until we all arrived at a point: This is the biggest thing that has ever happened in America in our lifetimes.

And, of course, the most horrible. The people who were killed that day were entirely innocent. None of the victims had been recruited to fight for anything. They were our neighbors, colleagues, friends and family—cut down for no evident reason. Those who did the killing tried to explain themselves to the world, their argument essentially distilling to: America is evil. The world at large rejected this rationale, and war was on. It was us against them, and never before had the United States been allied with so many.

Would Afghanistan be another Vietnam or, rather, a Grenada, a Kuwait? Short term, it seemed to be the latter. Long term is, now, in the hands of 2002, 2003 and all years yet to come.

Joe Raedle/Getty

Heating Up Below

In fact, new evidence showed that it's heating up all over.
While global warming could not be blamed for any
particular heat wave, drought or deluge, scientists on a U.N.-
sponsored panel said in March that a creep toward a warmer
world had begun. They pointed to melting glaciers, rising
oceans and extreme weather as signs of a dangerous trend
and said worldwide temperatures had climbed more than
1°F since 1900; the '90s were the hottest decade on record.
In Antarctica, home to these Adélie penguins, the annual
melt season has, in just 20 years, gotten three weeks longer.

Photograph by Tui de Roy/Minden Pictures

Winter

Bill's Final Bow

After delivering his farewell address to the nation, President Clinton bid adieu to his staff in the Oval Office. Thus closed a Presidency whose hallmarks were a booming national economy and constant scandal. Clinton's closing act, the granting of pardons, only furthered the latter legacy. Of 140 issued on Jan. 20, critics saw the case of billionaire financier Marc Rich as particularly egregious. Rich had fled a 1983 indictment on charges of tax evasion, fraud and "trading with the enemy" oil deals, and had since lived in Switzerland. After Clinton pardoned him, it was learned that Rich's ex-wife, Denise, had not only intervened in her former husband's behalf but had given $1 million to the Democratic Party, more than $100,000 to Hillary Clinton's successful run for Senate and $450,000 to the William J. Clinton Presidential Foundation in Little Rock, Ark.

Photograph by PF Bently PFPIX.COM

Jan. 1 According to most scholars, today marks the real dawning of **the new millennium.** Compared with 2000's lollapaloozas, the day proceeds quietly.

Jan. 2 As **the economy continues to falter,** layoffs increase while perks and salaries are being cut at many companies.

Jan. 9 Two noteworthy finds are announced by the **American Astronomical Society.** The first is a pair of planets about the mass of Jupiter that spin in perfect alignment around their home star, 15 light-years away. Second, and still more out of this world: a solar system 123 light-years distant, with one ordinary planet and another mysterious one 17 times as massive as Jupiter. Astronomer Geoffrey Marcy calls it "a bit frightening."

Jan. 13 Ronald Reagan, 89, in the grip of Alzheimer's, undergoes **successful surgery** after breaking his right hip.

An Earlier Horror

Afghanistan's year of living dangerously opened with the worst famine in 30 years. After a long drought in Badgis province, every well had run dry in the village where Hawaneen, a wispy-bearded patriarch (left), lived with his family. He sold his plow and set off for a refugee camp near Herat, where he found 80,000 others but few rations. Despite estimates that a million Afghans were at risk of starvation, few nations would donate to a country whose rulers harbored terrorists. After a month in camp, Hawaneen's son contracted pneumonia and died. The family looked on as a Muslim cleric laid the corpse on plastic and washed it for burial.

Photograph by Alexandra Boulat
VII for TIME

❝ Afghanistan is going through its worst crisis since the 1979 Soviet invasion, and nobody seems to care. ❞

—**U.N. relief official** stationed in Pakistan

Jan. 17 Jesse Jackson reveals that he has **fathered a daughter** outside of marriage and apologizes, saying that he will step back from public life, "to revive my spirit and reconnect with my family."

Jan. 20 Following in the footsteps of his father, **George W. Bush is inaugurated** as the 43rd President of the United States.

Jan. 24 Ending the **biggest manhunt since Bonnie and Clyde,** the last two of the "Malevolent Seven" convicts surrender to police in Colorado Springs, 42 days after escaping from a maximum-security prison outside San Antonio. Most of them had posed as Christian missionaries.

Jan. 26 A 7.9-magnitude earthquake hits western India, killing 13,000 to 15,000.

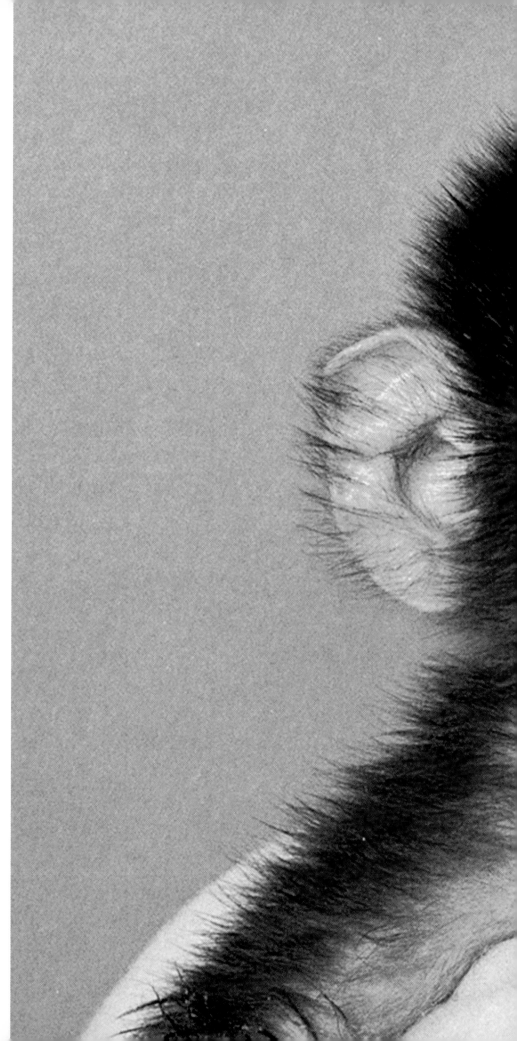

Genetic Monkey Business

On Jan. 11 scientists in Oregon announced the creation of the first genetically engineered monkey and introduced a rhesus named ANDi, backwards for "inserted DNA." The furry fellow sure looked simian but was at least a bit . . . jellyfish. His genesis: Researchers had stitched a jellyfish gene into a virus, infected 224 monkey eggs with the virus, fertilized the eggs, implanted 40 embryos in 20 females and then analyzed the three babies that were born. Only ANDi carried the extra gene throughout his body, but the implications in a species so close to human were immediately startling and, to many, troubling. Yes, gene manipulation might someday be used to fight illness. But what comes next?

Photograph Getty Reuters

"You could not morally justify attempting anything like this in humans for a very long time."

—**Tom Murray,** president of the Hastings Center for Bioethics

Jan. 26 Liv Ullmann and Ingmar Bergman reunite for a new film, *Faithless.* In a turnabout, she is the director, and he the writer and subject.

Jan. 27 After years of submersion in a morass of problems, **Jennifer Capriati** overcomes her personal devils, and Martina Hingis, to win the Australian Open, her first Grand Slam title.

Jan. 28 The Baltimore Ravens, led by MVP linebacker Ray Lewis, glide past the New York Giants, 34–7, in **Super Bowl XXXV.**

Feb. 4 *The Surrendered Wife* by Laura Doyle, which proposes that **a woman acquiesce** to her husband for the sake of their marriage, is a nonfiction best-seller.

A Going Concern

This boy looks out from his father's shop in Mbare, Zimbabwe. It is a coffin shop. Business has never been so good. Since the initial reported case of AIDS two decades ago, it has been a scourge that has spread across the entire globe, but nowhere are its withering, uncompromising results seen so commonly as in Africa. By the end of 2000, AIDS had killed 17 million people in sub-Saharan Africa, three times more than in the rest of the world. More than a million children under 15 were living with HIV, most having received the virus from their mothers. In this boy's land, Zimbabwe, one quarter of all adults were HIV-positive, and the epidemic was growing.

Photograph by Kristen Ashburn Contact

Feb. 9 *Hannibal* savors the third-biggest **box office** cash return in history, grossing $58 million the first weekend. The flick, with Anthony Hopkins as the epicurean title character, is based on the Thomas Harris best-seller.

Feb. 12 A San Francisco Court of Appeals rules that **Napster,** which permits free downloading of music from the Net, violates copyright laws.

Feb. 14 Reversing a 1999 ruling, the Kansas State Board of Education votes 7 to 3 to restore **the teaching of evolution** to the classroom.

Feb. 18 One of the **most feared sluggers** of the 1950s, Eddie Mathews, dies at age 69. The lefty-hitting third baseman struck 512 home runs over a 17-year career, 15 of them with the Braves, and was elected to baseball's Hall of Fame in 1978.

Feb. 18 FBI agent Robert Philip Hanssen is arrested and accused of having **spied for Moscow** since 1985. To avoid the death penalty he pleads guilty on July 6 to 15 counts of espionage and conspiracy.

Before Their Time

Not long ago, school was a sanctuary, a place of learning—book-learning, of course, but also learning how to get along with your peers. Here, in a too-familiar tableau, a 15-year-old girl was comforted after her school suffered the worst violence since Columbine. At Santana High in Santee, Calif., on March 5, 15-year-old Charles "Andy" Williams, who classmates said was the butt of jokes, began firing a .22-caliber revolver. Randy Gordon, 17, and Bryan Zuckor, 14, were slain. Eleven other students, a student teacher and a security guard were wounded. Days earlier, Williams had said he was going to "pull a Columbine." Nobody reported the threat.

Photograph by John Gastaldo
San Diego Union Tribune/Zuma Press

❝ I looked at the kid, and he was smiling and shooting his weapon. It was total chaos. People were trying to take cover. ❞
—**John Schardt,** 17

Feb. 26 The fanatic Taliban, which has ruled Afghanistan since 1996, orders the **destruction of all Buddhist statues,** including a 1,500-year-old figure carved into a mountainside. It was one of the country's few remaining treasures.

Feb. 28 The **Pacific Northwest** suffers a 6.8 earthquake that injures 200 and causes well over $2 billion in damages. Experts say the Big One is still to come.

March 7 Pharmaceutical giants slash prices of **AIDS drugs** as a result of pressure from generics.

March 7 "Over the Rainbow" is voted the **No. 1 song** of the century by the National Endowment of the Arts and the Recording Industry Association of America.

The Pursuit of Justice

Black-clad special-police forces stormed the Belgrade home of Slobodan Milosevic on March 31. Bystanders heard gunfire outside the house, then shots from within. On June 29 the archnationalist Serbian was incarcerated in The Hague on charges of war crimes committed against ethnic Albanians during the brutal 1999 conflict in Kosovo. Four months later he was accused of committing murder and atrocities in Croatia in 1991. Milosevic is the first elected head of state to be transferred by a government to an international war crimes tribunal. His trial is scheduled for Feb. 12, 2002.

Photograph by Ivan Milutinovic
Getty Reuters

March 7 The Dallas Cowboys choose not to renew the contract of three-time Super Bowl–winning **quarterback Troy Aikman.** The 34-year-old has had 10 concussions.

March 9 The stock price of **Internet icon Yahoo** drops to $17 from a high of $216.34 at the end of December 1999.

March 19 More than a million customers face losing their electricity in California as power-grid managers order blackouts after **electricity reserves fall almost to zero.** At four hours, the outages are twice as long as those in January.

March 23 After 15 often-turbulent years in orbit, the Russian space station *Mir* returns to Earth amid fears that the 135-ton complex might break up in a rain of destruction. However, **the splashdown in the South Pacific** proves to be uneventful. The Russians were forced to bring *Mir* down because they could no longer bankroll a superpower-size space program.

March 25 *Gladiator* snares five **Oscars,** including Best Picture and Actor (Russell Crowe). *Erin Brockovich* star Julia Roberts takes home the statuette for Best Actress.

The First 100 Days

It is standard to use the winter months of a new President's tenure as a measuring stick. The honeymoon ends as pundits and the public ask: How's he doing? How will he do tomorrow?

Doug Mills/AP

Eric Draper/The White House

The peaceful transfer of authority is rare in history, yet common in our country." This observation, from the opening of George W. Bush's Inaugural Address on Jan. 20, was decidedly germane. For one thing, very few nations can boast of centuries of orderly progression. But also, this particular accession of authority had been preceded by months of nation-splitting rancor. Inflamed by a proliferating argot of dimpled and pregnant chads, partisan allegiance had turned incendiary. One man emerged, and now he was sworn in. What next?

There is, in the United States, a tradition for answering that question, for framing that early assessment. In 1933, Franklin D. Roosevelt became Chief Executive at a time of genuine crisis, characterized by deep concerns about the survival of democratic capitalism and the office itself. He

The 43rd President of the United States is sworn in by Chief Justice William Rehnquist as family, friends and colleagues look on. At right, President Bush and Vice President Dick Cheney get in sync in the Oval Office after the swearing-in of Secretary of State Colin Powell on Jan. 26.

responded by assaulting the tyranny of Depression with a wave of reform bills, passed by Congress, often with barely a glance. Ever since, once a President has completed his first 100 days, it is customary to take off the blinders and appraise the initial success, or lack thereof.

For President Bush, his first 100 days transpired in an atmosphere of relative calm, and his performance was in general regarded as, if not tremendously productive, at least benign. The nagging concern about the man, except among his most ardent supporters, had been in the area of substance. Early in 2001, the country seemed to give him a pass on this issue. Okay, he wasn't a great orator; but while honed speaking skills are certainly desirable in a leader, they don't constitute a sine qua non. His

grasp of who was the pasha or sultan of some faraway nation—say, Pakistan—was questioned; well, not everyone knows the answers to such arcane queries. The new Chief Executive's grasp of history was described as tenuous at best; well, hey, school is out. The important news was that the man had aced the biggest test of them all by surrounding himself with a cabinet of experienced, sober people who could answer these sorts of questions, and would know how to articulate them to the man in the Oval Office.

In his first 100 days the new President wasn't confronted by any earth-shattering decisions and, without a trial by fire, the overall response of the public was let's wait and see. The wait would not be a long one.

Win McNamee/Getty Reuters

Eric Draper/The White House

Eric Draper/The White House

Clockwise from top right: On Inauguration Day, the new Chief Executive test-drives the Oval Office that his father manned for four years; two days later, Secretary of State–designate Powell confers with the President in the same august room; at the Capitol on Feb. 27, Bush shakes hands after addressing a joint session of Congress.

tickets than any other pro sport; NASCAR's got a huge new network contract; NASCAR's zooming. But until Earnhardt crashed, the true reach of NASCAR and its hold on the fanship—NASCAR Nation is as much culture as sport—wasn't fully understood. Now it is.

What about the man? He was the perfect blend of tradition and today to bring NASCAR to the front page. Born in Kannapolis, N.C., in 1951, he didn't take naturally to school—he would drop out in the ninth grade—but loved being around cars. His dad, Ralph, known as Ironheart, was a short-track racing god and taught his son to wrangle a stock car. Meanwhile, NASCAR was organizing itself around a nucleus of 15 to 20 drivers who were of a type: rugged, poor or near poor, exclusively southern, fearless. It had grown to be more than a semi-slick operation by the time Earnhardt joined the carnival in 1979, and when he started winning everything in sight—11 races one year, nine in another—NASCAR was in a position to make him a bona fide sports superstar. Earnhardt, for his part, took NASCAR to another level with his flat-out, peerless driving. He did it again with his death.

Rarely has a man's legacy been so direct or touching: After finishing second on the day his father died, Dale Earnhardt Jr. went on to win three NASCAR races in the 2001 campaign, including the circuit's midsummer return to fateful Daytona.

Fathers and sons: Dale's dad taught him to drive, and Dale handed the wheel to his son. Only a week after No. 3 (right) crashed, Dale Jr. donned a helmet and was back in his own car for a race in Rockingham, N.C. Ironhead, Ironheart's boy, would surely have been proud.

Spring

Unbottled Water

Some of the worst flooding since 1920 spread across much of the upper half of France early in the year, creating miserable and dangerous conditions. Here, swollen rivers in the Breton town of Quimperle crashed over their banks, bringing furious floods through this and neighboring communities. Fifty-four towns in the Somme Valley were underwater, and in Paris the Île de la Cité was covered in brown water for days. The flooding was blamed on an unusually mild and rainy winter.

Photograph by Demange-LeBot/Gamma

Amexica

The U.S. population along the Mexican border is growing at almost twice the national rate, and an unofficial cross-border republic of 24 million Americans and Mexicans now draws influence from both nations. On a typical day a million barrels of crude oil, 432 tons of bell peppers and $51 million in auto parts arrive from Mexico, as do thousands of border jumpers, like this one in Agua Prieta. An average of 4,600 are caught daily, but illegal Mexicans in the U.S. now total three million. This isn't lost on President Bush, who invited Mexico's Vincente Fox to be the first foreign leader to make an official state visit. Later, Fox asked that the illegals be allowed to stay in the U.S., and Bush promised to work with Congress on a new immigration policy.

Photograph by Alex Webb Magnum

April 1 The pilot of an American EP-3E spy plane, Lt. Shane Osborn, **brilliantly saves the craft from crashing** when it is forced down by Chinese fighters, one of which crashes. China demands an apology, and the U.S., after 11 days of diplomatic jousting, offers its regrets. Following the standoff, the 24 crewmembers return home to a heroes' welcome. The stripped-down fuselage of the plane is not returned to the U.S. until three months later.

April 8 In a tense showdown with David Duval and Phil Mickelson, Tiger Woods wins the Masters by two strokes. It is the fourth consecutive major victory for Woods, who, along with many others, considers it a **Grand Slam.** Dissenters claim that all four majors must be won in a calendar year for it to constitute a Slam.

April 20 An American **missionary and her infant daughter** are killed when their plane is shot down by a Peruvian Air Force jet that suspects the plane of carrying drugs. Language barriers are blamed.

The Buck Stops Here

Navy Commander Scott Daniel Waddle shed a tear in his home in Pearl Harbor on April 11 as he relived his fateful tale. On Feb. 9, Waddle was the skipper of the nuclear submarine USS *Greeneville,* which was on a voyage off Oahu as part of a distinguished-visitor program that lets civilians ride around on Naval vessels. In a freak accident, the sub struck and sank the *Ehime Maru,* a Japanese fisheries-training ship, killing nine. The incident brought torrid criticism from Tokyo and led to a series of U.S. apologies. Waddle later retired, with full rank and pension, after an inquiry concluded that he had neglected proper and safe procedures.

Photograph by Steve Liss

> **❝ I know this fine American patriot feels terrible about what took place. It was a terrible accident, and like any good commander he's taking the heat. He is taking the hit. ❞**
>
> —**President George W. Bush**

April 24 Struggling with the worst economic scenario since World War II, **Japan elects a new prime minister,** Junichiro Koizumi. The 59-year-old maverick politician, who features long wavy hair and enjoys both heavy metal and Puccini, vows to "change Japan."

April 24 The Supreme Court rules that police have the authority to arrest and jail people who have broken even minor laws. The 5-to-4 verdict upholds the 1997 hourlong **jailing of a Texas mother** for not using seatbelts for herself or her two small children. Gail Atwater had claimed she let the kids take off their belts to look for a toy on the way home from soccer practice.

That Others May Live

This tragic, necessary pyre in the town of Wreay in England's north country was part of a desperate attempt to contain an outbreak of foot-and-mouth disease. Only one member of this herd of cattle needed to contract the disease. The virus spreads so rapidly that there is no culling out: All must be destroyed. The British livestock industry was already on the ropes from mad cow disease, swine flu and winter flooding when foot-and-mouth—which also affects pigs, sheep and goats but not humans or horses—was spotted in an Essex slaughterhouse on Feb. 20. The next day the nation was forced to halt exports of animals, meat and milk. In the following months, millions of creatures and billions of dollars were lost as the disease hit such countries as France and Argentina. In the United States, officials responded promptly to the threat, and no evidence of the disease was seen here.

Photograph by Mark Pinder Gamma

April 26 Former Senator and Medal of Honor winner Bob Kerrey acknowledges that a Navy SEAL team he led in a 1969 raid in Vietnam **killed women and children.** Kerrey, who admits feeling "guilty about what happened," says the unit fired only after being fired on in a zone that had previously been cleared of civilians. Accounts of the incident vary.

April 30 Twenty-four-year-old **Chandra Levy** is seen for the last time at a Washington, D.C., health club. The disappearance of Levy, an intern for Congressman Gary Condit, 53, is steady headline fodder for months.

May 6 Sixty-year-old Dennis Tito comes back to Earth after his $20 million **space vacation** on a Russian *Soyuz* taxi mission.

Camelot Redux

"Jacqueline Kennedy: the White House Years" began a three-month run at New York's Metropolitan Museum of Art in May. The collection of more than 80 classic '60s outfits worn by the late First Lady was one of the most de rigueur shows at the Met in decades, drawing 559,000 rapt attendees who were reminded—or quickly learned—what a bright, flawless sense of style she possessed, and why she was such a pervasive influence. It was a good year for things Jackie. Besides her pillbox hats and sleeveless A-lines, a selection of her favorite poems also fared well.

Photograph by Catuffe Sipa

> **" Jacqueline Kennedy is one of history's great style icons. "**
>
> —**Hamish Bowles,**
> guest curator of the exhibit

May 7 Leaders of Cincinnati's black community call for calm after a grand jury returns two misdemeanor charges against a white police officer who fatally shot a 19-year-old black man on April 7. **The slaying of Timothy Thomas,** the 16th black since 1995 to be shot while being apprehended by Cincinnati police, had triggered the worst racial unrest there since 1968.

May 25 With its $140 million budget, the biggest ever green-lighted for a movie, *Pearl Harbor* opens to tepid reviews (*Time* calls it "watchable in a dim, beclouded sort of way") but an explosive box office.

June 6 An L.A. jury awards 56-year-old Richard Boeken $3 billion in his suit against Philip Morris. The lawyer for the former **two-pack-a-day smoker** said the company portrayed smoking as "cool." On Aug. 15, Boeken settles for $100 million.

Death in Kathmandu

In a farewell ceremony of the highest magnitude, crowds gathered on the banks of the sacred Bagmati River on June 2 for the cremation of the Nepalese royal family. It was just one day after the worst mass murder of royalty since the 1918 Bolshevik slaying of the Russian tsar and his kin. In a bizarre scene at the Nepalese palace, Crown Prince Dipendra Bir Bikram allegedly shot and killed his father, King Birendra, his mother, Queen Aishwarya, and seven other royals before taking his own life. Days later Prince Gyanendra, the uncle of the shooter, was named as the nation's new king. Gyanendra called the shooting "accidental."

Photograph by Reglain Frederic Gamma

June 18 Pulitzer Prize–winning historian Joseph J. Ellis confesses that he **lied to his Mount Holyoke students** about being an airborne soldier in Vietnam. His service time was actually spent teaching history at West Point. Ellis is suspended from his teaching post for one year without pay.

June 20 Andrea Yates calls Houston police to report the drowning deaths of her five children, ages six months to seven years. When an officer arrives, she reportedly says, **"I killed my children."** According to her husband, the 37-year-old housewife has been "withdrawn" and "robotic" because of severe postpartum depression and her father's recent death.

June 22 For the first time in 17 years, a **California condor is born in the wild.** The egg had been laid in the Los Angeles Zoo, then rushed to the Los Padres National Forest just days before the due date. The chick emerged with the aid of its foster condor mother, who knew just what to do.

Facing the Music

On June 6, Bill McVeigh of Pendleton, N.Y., was doing exactly what millions of other Americans were doing: sitting in his living room watching the news on television. The big difference was that he was looking at his son, Timothy, a 33-year-old terrorist who had killed 168 people at an Oklahoma City federal building in 1995. Five days after this photo was taken, McVeigh was executed in Terre Haute, Ind. There had been an earlier delay when the FBI, in an embarrassing revelation, said that it had failed to turn over 3,135 documents in the case, but the lethal injection would finally be administered, the act itself carried on closed-circuit TV.

Photograph by David Duprey AP

❝ We didn't get anything. ❞

—**Paul Howell,** whose 27-year-old daughter died in the bombing, after McVeigh showed no sign of contrition

June 25 The New York Assembly votes 125 to 19 to **ban the use of handheld cell phones** while driving. The state becomes the first to pass such a bill, which will go into effect on November 1. Says Assembly speaker Sheldon Silver: "This is going to save lives, I'm sure."

June 30 Vice President Dick Cheney, 60, receives a sophisticated **pacemaker and defibrillator** implant in his chest. This, his third major procedure since being elected, is designed to modify an irregular heartbeat. He returns to work two days later, joking, "I'm told it's already an energy-efficient device."

On screen: BREAKING NEWS — JUDGE DENIES STAY IN MCVEIGH EXECUTION — NAS 9.68 — 10:25 PT

The Arctic Refuge

In a strange and beautiful land at the top of Alaska, the rivers flow north out of the majestic Brooks Range and into the serene tundra by the sea. That's where controversy lies buried.

Art Wolfe

I t all had an eerie sense of déjà vu. President Bush pushing—hard—to allow oil drilling in a magnificent American wilderness, Alaska's Arctic National Wildlife Refuge, citing a national energy crisis as rationale and setting off a tundra war with environmentalists. The scenario was played out in 1991 when George Bush père, despite the threat posed to oil stocks by the Gulf War, was unable to muster sufficient Congressional support for opening up the refuge. It was played out again in 2001 when George W. Bush, despite rolling blackouts in California, similarly could not spur a legislative oil rush. Now, of course, with America's relationship to the petroleum-rich Middle East complicated beyond measure, more fluid than the black gold in a pipeline, one thing only is certain: The country is by no means finished with its war over ANWR.

What is this place, and what is the issue? The Arctic National Wildlife Refuge is an exotic 18.9-million-acre tract in the northeast corner of Alaska, a place of mountains and rivers sweeping down to a vast coastal plain. The biggest oil strike in U.S. history—more than 10 billion barrels to date—was made in 1968 at Prudhoe Bay, just west of ANWR. For decades, oilmen have speculated that an equally immense store lies buried beneath the refuge.

The place, so very remote and for much of the year so climatically hostile, is rarely visited by man.

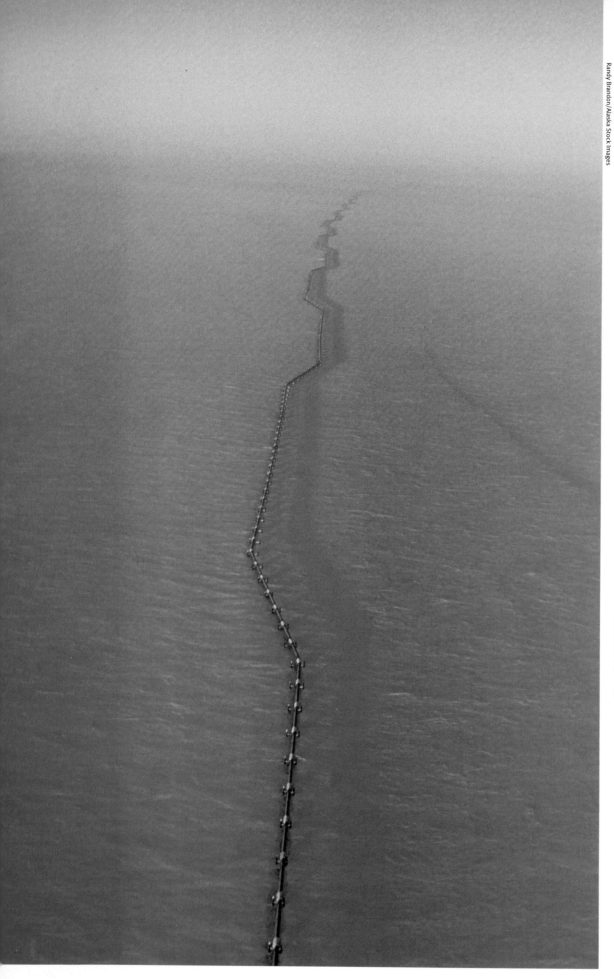

Proponents of drilling in ANWR say the Trans-Alaska pipeline running south from Prudhoe Bay hasn't disturbed wildlife, while opponents say the entire operation at Prudhoe has been an environmental disaster, with seepages poisoning land and water. Musk oxen and the Porcupine caribou herd of the Arctic Refuge haven't been polled on the matter.

But it is home to an astonishing variety of flora and fauna. Dall sheep browse in the foothills of the Brooks Range as eagles soar above. Grizzly bears prowl, musk oxen graze and, down by the sea in calving season—right where the drilling would be—the great Porcupine caribou herd welcomes thousands of newborn each year.

Would-be developers believe that the technology of oil prospecting is so advanced the terrain would barely be touched. Those who would preserve ANWR as it is say industry is never green, and the animals' rhythms would be critically disrupted. We heard all this in 1991, in 2001, and we'll hear it again. Events unfolding half a world away assure: We will hear all this again.

Gary Braasch/Woodfin Camp

PORTRAIT | Julia Roberts

It was the year when this winsome beauty with the intergalactic smile and the smattering of exes finally staked her claim at the top of Mount Hollywood.

Timothy White/Corbis Outline

S he was a box office smash at age 22, and at 34, she is the biggest woman star in the world. What's more, she seems like someone who will never age, or misplace her joie de vivre. Julia Roberts reigns as America's Sweetheart—who else could even pretend to that throne?— and the year 2001 bestowed the crowning glory.

It is a success saga with a bumpy beginning. Born in Smyrna, Ga., on Oct. 28, 1967, Julie Fiona Roberts was four when her parents, who ran an unsuccessful acting workshop out of their Atlanta home, divorced. In high school she played tennis and developed an interest in literature (today she reads Whitman, Faulkner and Hardy). There was no drama department at her school, but after graduating, she followed in the thespian footsteps of her older brother, Eric, and set off for New York.

Good fortune came quickly. In 1988 she snagged a spicy role in *Mystic Pizza*, and she registered the next year as Sally Field's fragile daughter in *Steel Magnolias*. Then her genuine, glorious smile and irresistible charm conquered the world—$463 million earned globally—in *Pretty Woman*, whose director, Garry Marshall, sized her up nicely when he told *People,* "Julia is a cross between Audrey Hepburn, Lucille Ball and Bambi."

Actresses come and go, but only a few linger in the memory. Roberts is one of that rare breed. She is beautiful, but in her own fashion; graceful, but a little bit gawky, too; smart, but not in-your-face about it; when it comes to talent, she simply makes it look easy.

In the realm of romantic comedy, she is anyone's equal, glittering in *My Best Friend's Wedding, Notting Hill* and *Runaway Bride*, huge hits all. But Hollywood likes to reserve its highest honor for big dramas, and it took the story of a single mom battling powerful interests for Roberts to score the Academy Award for Best Actress. Accepting the prize for *Erin Brockovich* in vintage black-and-white velvet Valentino, Roberts crowed "I love the world" and

SPRING **LIFE** 51

thanked "everyone I've ever met in my life." It was a very Julia moment.

After her giddy spring fling with Oscar, she was back at work, re-teaming with *Brockovich* director Steven Soderbergh on the high-profile remake of *Ocean's Eleven*, which opened in December. By all accounts she and *Ocean*'s other megawatt stars—George Clooney, Matt Damon, Brad Pitt and Andy Garcia—had a gay old time on the set, pranks a-plenty. But of course, in the real world, as in the reel world, not every moment is sublime—and Roberts had her sad times in 2001 as well. Through the years, she has been involved in a lot of romantic fizzles: Liam Neeson, Dylan McDermott, Daniel Day-Lewis, a dumped-at-the-aisle Kiefer Sutherland, a divorced husband in Lyle Lovett. This year her four-year relationship with actor Benjamin Bratt closed down. Unlucky-in-love seems to be part of the territory when you're the Queen of the Box Office, as does the attendant gossip. Roberts wishes quietly that people would mind their own beeswax. But when it comes to her, that's not so easy. As Diane Sawyer once observed, "There's something too magical in her to ignore."

Bob Marshak/Universal

Roberts has clicked with some high-voltage costars in her recent celluloid outings (clockwise from above): Albert Finney in her Oscar-winner, *Erin Brockovich;* John Cusack in *America's Sweethearts;* Andy Garcia and George Clooney in *Ocean's Eleven;* and Brad Pitt in *The Mexican.*

Photofest (2)

Bob Marshak/Warner Bros.

Kevork Djansezian/AP

Beware of Darkness

On June 21, the very first day of summer (well, it was the beginning of winter in southern Africa), these Zimbabwean children took proper precautions as they prepared to watch the earth's first total solar eclipse of the millennium. When the moon blocked rays of the sun for three minutes, the sky darkened to twilight as planets and stars appeared. It was noted by Peter Sibanda, spokesman for the National Traditional Healers Association, that local legend held the periodic "rotting of the sun" was God's way of heralding "upcoming problems, death, illness, drought or incurable diseases." As the eclipse traveled across central Africa, one was left to wonder what more could befall a continent already visited by all of these plagues.

Photograph by Howard Burditt
Getty Reuters

Summer

Another Hot Year

The Italians can count on it: Mount Etna in Sicily, Europe's most active volcano, will be as sizzling in its season as the fashion shows of Milan. A strong eruptive episode in May triggered volcanism that continued throughout the summer, with lava fountains rising hundreds of feet above their vents and Strombolian bursts sending incandescent bombs more than 500 yards above the crater rim. Ash coated the towns of Giarre and Catania, and on July 22, earth barriers were constructed as lava flows threatened buildings. There were no fatalities, although one gawker who got too close fell and broke his back while running from the lava.

Photograph by Spot Image Gamma

July 3 Surgeons in Louisville, Ky., announce that they have implanted the **first artificial heart** in a human being. When the anesthesia for the procedure, which involved a two-pound, battery-driven heart, wore off, recipient Robert Tools, 59, said he had to smile because "I saw people, not the heavenly host."

July 9 Croatian Goran Ivanisevic wins his first **Wimbledon** championship, defeating Patrick Rafter of Australia in five sets. The women's title is retained by America's Venus Williams, who beats Justine Henin of Belgium in three sets for her second consecutive Wimbledon crown.

July 10 At the baseball **All-Star Game** in Seattle, the American League chalks up a 4–1 victory. Cal Ripken Jr., in his 18th and final All-Star competition, is named MVP.

Say It Ain't So

Felipe Almonte came to the U.S. from the Dominican Republic in June 2000 with his son Danny, who soon started pitching for a Little League team in New York City's the Bronx. Danny had uncommon ability, and in 2001 was the star of the Rolando Paulino All-Stars, even pitching a perfect game in the first round of the Little League World Series. But suspicions about his age were confirmed when a *Sports Illustrated* reporter unearthed a copy of a birth certificate in Danny's hometown that proved the boy to be 14 years old—two years too old for Little League. A tale of glory turned to disgrace as Paulino and Danny's dad were barred from Little League for life. Danny's team had to forfeit its wins.

Photograph by Mike Segar Getty Reuters

❝ Clearly adults have used Danny Almonte in a most contemptible and despicable way. Their actions are reprehensible. ❞

—**Stephen D. Keener,** CEO and president of Little League Baseball

Aug. 2 The Senate quickly and unanimously confirms veteran prosecutor Robert S. Mueller III as **top cop at the FBI.** The former Marine faces a tough challenge at the troubled agency.

Aug. 6 Alfred A. Knopf agrees to pay former President Bill Clinton more than $10 million for his **memoirs.**

Aug. 8 American Fulbright scholar John E. Tobin Jr. returns from a six-month term in a **Russian jail** for marijuana possession. Tobin had been accused of espionage but never charged with it.

Give Me Your Tired

At the dedication of the Statue of Liberty on October 28, 1886, President Grover Cleveland, on behalf of the United States, accepted the great gift from France, saying, "We will not forget that Liberty has here made her home; nor shall her chosen altar be neglected." Well, certainly, worship can take different paths. On Aug. 23, for Frenchman Thierry Devaux, it meant using a parachute and gas-powered propeller. The 41-year-old daredevil apparently forgot, however, that the long arm of the law reacheth out even in a free world. While police officers were untangling Devaux, Lady Liberty had to be shut down for three hours. Nineteen days later, she would be shuttered indefinitely.

Photographs by Peter Morgan
Getty Reuters

Aug. 12 In a deal that could cost $1 billion, **Ford agrees to settle** a lawsuit alleging that faulty ignition systems in millions of cars could cause stalling.

Aug. 13 The first Bridgestone-Firestone trial begins in McAllen, Tex. Their **tires** have been associated with 203 deaths and more than 700 injuries.

Sept. 8 Laura Bush opens the first **National Book Festival** in Washington. The former librarian assembles a diverse group of writers to read from their books.

Sept. 9 *Band of Brothers,* based on Stephen E. Ambrose's tale of **an Army company in France on D-Day,** debuts on HBO. Tom Hanks and Steven Spielberg collaborated on the 10-hour miniseries.

Sept. 11 At 6:33 a.m., the sun rises over **New York City.**

This tableau has emerged as one of September 11's most iconic. The firefighters here and in the companion photo on this book's cover—seen from an angle that so recalls Iwo Jima in WWII—proudly, defiantly raise Old Glory.

FOCUS ON # September 11

A half century ago, America was attacked by the Japanese, who bequeathed the United States a date that would live in infamy. A half century after Pearl Harbor, an assault different in every way except for the element of surprise greeted a country that was awakening to what it assumed to be a peaceful day. In 1941, a sleeping giant stirred itself and went to meet the enemy. In the days after September 11, 2001, the United States again declared war.

Before the Storm

It is 8:47 a.m. Eastern Daylight Saving Time. American Airlines Flight 11 from Boston to Los Angeles, carrying 92 people and 20,000 gallons of jet fuel, is bearing down on the north tower of New York City's World Trade Center. The wing tip of the plane can be seen at left, behind the building. This is the first ominous glimpse of a terrible nightmare that roared into our lives when (opposite) the airliner rammed the north tower.

Clearly, the country was not prepared. We can anticipate much more quarreling about culpability in this lack of preparedness. But it needs to be remembered that September 11 was a wholly transforming day. At nightfall on September 10, America could see nothing on the horizon that said "Beware." The morning of September 11 was not like the dawn of December 7, 1941, when the country was already tearing itself apart over the question of isolationism, as the Nazi march through Europe and Japanese expansionism had the entire world—America included—wondering what was next, preparing for what was next. This was a September day in a nothing-happening year in a country that hadn't been attacked on its own ground in more than a half century, and hadn't seen blood spilled in wartime on its continental soil since its own civil conflict 136 years prior. Yes, this was, perhaps, a complacent country. But it was a country with such a long history of peace within its borders that it was all but impossible to be at the ready.

Signs were missed, no question. Terrorists of a like mindset to those who went into action on September 11 had already taken a shot at the World Trade Center in New York City. The 1993 attack, in which bombs were detonated in a parking garage, killed six and led to life terms for six Islamic extremists . . . American embassies had been bombed in Africa . . . Another radical Islamist had been caught after crossing the Canadian border just prior to the great millennium celebrations. It was learned that he was intent on bombing Los Angeles International Airport . . . In the year 2000, an American destroyer, the USS *Cole,* had been bombed while refueling in Yemen . . . And it eventuated that there were terrorists walking among us in recent months who were taking flying lessons, while not seeming keen to learn very much about takeoff or landing. Signs were missed.

Even if they hadn't been, there is no supposing that the terrorists might have been foiled, for what

An Evil Scenario

As the great city—and much of a nation watching live on television—tries to come to grips with what seems a terrible accident, a second malign image appears, the hijacked United Flight 175 from Boston, with 56 passengers and nine crewmembers.

they did at bottom was, simply, to exploit America's freedoms. In the land of the free, where individuals can come and go, where rights of movement and privacy are protected, they took advantage. They crossed borders and entered a nation that holds paramount freedom of speech, assembly and religion (in a horrible irony, a nation that since its inception has defended an individual's right to worship as he will). Then they attacked from within.

They did so on a day that, were it not destined to be remembered as one of the most horrible in America's history, might have been recalled, on the East Coast at least, as another perfect day in a glorious month. They did so on September 11, beginning before dawn. At 5:45 a.m., Mohamed Atta, as much of a ringleader as the gang had in the States, and Abdulaziz Alomari passed through security in Portland, Me., and boarded a commuter flight to Boston. Also heading for Logan International Airport were their confederates Waleed M. Alshehri, Satam Al Suqami and Wail Alshehri. Those five would board American Flight 11 bound for Los Angeles. Five others were also at Logan that morning. Their flight, United 175, also destined for L.A., took off 14 minutes after the American jet, and by 8:15 a.m., 127 other passengers, 20 crewmembers and the 10 hijackers were aloft.

Meantime, in Washington, American Flight 77 for Los Angeles was boarding at Dulles International Airport. In Newark, N.J., United Flight 93 for San Francisco was doing the same. The former had 58 passengers aboard—among them, five hijackers—and the latter had 37 passengers, including four hijackers. Within four minutes of Flight 93's takeoff at 8:42, the North American Aerospace Defense Command (NORAD), reacting to notification by the Federal Aviation Administration, was scrambling F-15 fighter planes at the Otis Air National Guard Base on Cape Cod to overtake two planes that, apparently, had been hijacked after leaving Boston.

Too late. The American Airlines plane, having veered north to Albany before barreling down the

9:02 EDT

The south tower of the Trade Center, wrapped in smoke from its twin, is blasted into by the United plane, which resembles nothing so much as a missile. The impact and the fuel from the Boeing 767 airliner sets off an inferno of hellacious intensity and spews metal, glass and concrete far out over the bustling blocks below.

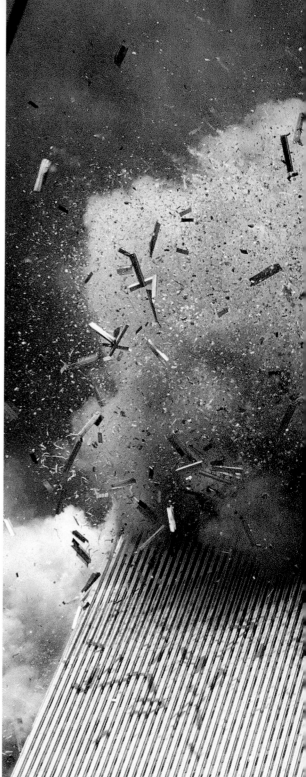

Rob Howard

Naomi Stock/TimePix

Hudson River Valley, slammed into the north tower of the World Trade Center at 8:47 a.m. The crash destroyed much of floors 90 through 100, and set off a conflagration fed by 20,000 gallons of jet fuel. As horror engulfed lower Manhattan, word spread throughout the city. Some old-timers and history buffs, recalling the B-25 bomber that got lost in the fog and crashed into the 79th floor of the Empire State Building in 1945, wondered if another terri-

ble accident had happened. Those thoughts vanished instantly at 9:02 when the United plane out of Boston came rushing in from a southern approach and blasted into the other tower, obliterating much of floors 78 to 87. Three minutes later White House Chief of Staff Andrew Card interrupted President George W. Bush for a second time during an appearance before a second-grade class in Sarasota, Fla., and it was clear to both men that the

day, the nation and indeed the world order had changed irrevocably.

By 10 a.m. Eastern Daylight Time: All bridges and tunnels into New York City were closed; the New York Stock Exchange had suspended trading; for the first time in history, the FAA ordered all non-military planes grounded and canceled all flights in the U.S.; the airspace over New York City is sterilized; New York Mayor Rudolph W. Giuliani was on the scene downtown, taking charge, at one point dodging debris; Bush had told the nation, "We have had a national tragedy. Two airplanes have crashed into the World Trade Center in an apparent terrorist attack on our country"; all U.S. financial markets were closed; the White House and U.S. Capitol were evacuated; the President had departed Florida on an evasive route to Barksdale Air Force Base outside Shreveport, La.

And, at 9:41, American Flight 77, having swung around after leaving Dulles, crashed into the Pentagon building, the nerve center of the U.S. military. And, at 9:50, the 110-story south tower of the World Trade Center collapsed, imploding and sending through the canyons of lower Manhattan a thick cloud of ash and smoke, and upon the Hudson River a blizzard of office paper.

These earliest hours of the day's tick-tock are laid out here in some specificity to give a sense of how fast things were happening, and in how many places. The scrambled fighter planes were eight minutes behind the United jet as it completed the day's malevolent work in New York, and twelve minutes shy of intercepting the airliner that struck the Pentagon. They were in the air on highest alert waiting for anything else incoming to Washington when United Flight 93, which had swept west as far as Cleveland before changing its direction and

heading for the nation's capital, mysteriously crashed in a field outside Shanksville, Pa. That happened at 10 a.m., and within a half hour the other Twin Tower had collapsed.

So, then: Much of what you see on these pages happened very quickly, and the subsequent images and their accompanying information take you through the rest of what is one of the worst, most horrific, most spectacular, most profoundly sad months in our country's history. For three jittery weeks, evidence of what had happened behind the scenes on September 11 was uncovered, even as there were new developments—new news. The American on the street became all too familiar with a repressive Afghani regime known as the Taliban, a group of extremely fundamentalist Islamists who certainly were harboring terrorists, most prominent among these Osama bin Laden, the prime suspect in the September 11 attacks, and were also perse-

A Disturbing Report
President Bush, in a Sarasota, Fla., school to promote his education program, hears at 9:05 the unthinkable from White House Chief of Staff Andrew Card: A second plane has hit the Trade Center.

Brian C. Manning

Silhouette of Doom
The swath of a plane is evident in this shot from a nearby rooftop. Within the wreckage, a person signals for help. Below, firefighter Mike Kehoe wades through evacuees as he climbs toward trouble in the north tower. He was lucky to get out alive.

John Labriola

cuting women—at least as judged by any standard of morality but their own. Other news: The President gave a speech on September 20, the best speech of his life, that served to shore up American resolve, and then the big ships started streaming to the Middle East, their fighter planes fueled and ready. It quickly became clear that whether and when Afghanistan would be bombed was in the hands of the Taliban, and it became evident that bombing was imminent.

Stories came out. Through cell phone calls made from the plane, we learned that four or more passengers, in an extraordinary act of courage, had stormed the cabin and taken back the fate of Flight 93 somewhere over the hills of western Pennsylvania. We learned of countless acts of selfless heroism at the Trade Center, too many of the heroes no longer alive to accept thanks or acclaim. We learned that the teachers at the childcare center near the Pentagon had gotten every single preschooler and infant to safety, as had their counterparts at the WTC children's center.

Mark Stahl

The Nightmare Continues

Less than an hour after the first plane hit, a flight from D.C. to L.A. strikes the Pentagon, collapsing part of it. Above: At about 10:00, yet another plane crashes, in Pennsylvania. Heroic passengers fought the hijackers and averted an even worse disaster.

It seemed, for a brief time, as if the future held only this piecing-together of the events of September 11, soon to be accompanied by a war Over There. Then, on September 30, the news told us that a man from Florida was ill with inhaled anthrax. This had been one of those diseases cited by the newsweeklies as a possible next weapon for terrorists: dirty bombs, smallpox, anthrax. Inhalation anthrax in humans hadn't occurred in the U.S. since 1976. Investigators seemed to downplay things at first, looking into the man's travels to North Carolina, citing the man's love of nature. (Maybe he got it from animals?) But as September ended, the United States was beyond wary—it was scared.

October would bring war and more death— death in Afghanistan and death in America. But this story, in the history books, would never be about that. In a way more pronounced and forceful than even December 7, 1941, the original date of infamy, this would be about an abrupt reversal, a complete realignment of attitudes, beliefs and expectations. About a day so stunning in its implications that the world was turned upside down. It would not be about what was to follow; it would always be about September 11, a day so beautiful and innocent—so naive?—in its earliest moments. So black in its last. A day unlike any other, ever.

Daryl Donley/Sipa

The Unthinkable
The Twin Towers were built to withstand an impact from jetliners with fuel capacities as they existed when the towers were designed in the 1960s. The torrid temperatures that result from today's crash outstrip long-ago safety measures, causing the steel frame of the south tower to melt. The tower collapses at 9:50.

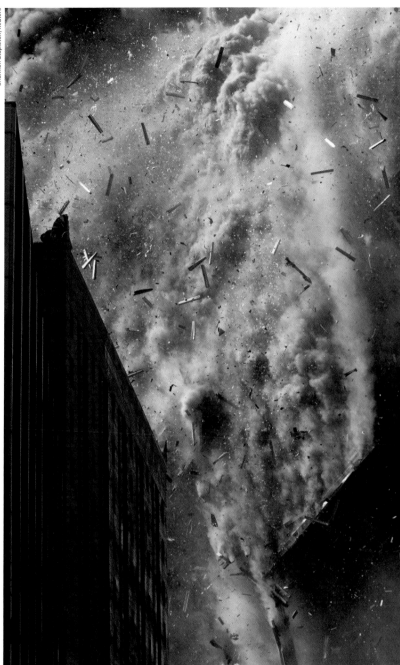

Spellbound

With the Municipal Building in
the rear, stunned and frightened
onlookers in lower Manhattan
watch the dreadful spectacle of
the south tower falling. Witnesses
report a tremendous sucking
sound followed by a powerful surge
of air as the floors descend.
A staggering, dense billow of dust,
dirt and debris congeals in the
catastrophic event and spreads
away from the building.

Cataclysm

At 10:28, just 38 minutes after the demise of its twin, the north tower collapses into itself in a scene of terrifying intensity. The already suffocating atmosphere is deluged with still more dust and debris. Although many workers had been evacuated, the death toll is high.

Steve McCurry/Magnum (4)

Flight

On the day of the attack, New Yorkers face situations that would test the mettle of anyone. Above, with public transportation hopelessly snarled, an endless stream of Brooklynites make their laborious way out of Manhattan via the Brooklyn Bridge. Many won't reach their homes until well into the night. The couple at left help each other through an unforgettable experience. People rarely panic, except, as opposite, when confronted by a moment of catastrophe right out of a horror movie.

Bound for a Martyr's Grave

The body of 68-year-old Mychal Judge, the chaplain of the New York Fire Department, is carried from the site. He had been administering last rites to a firefighter slain by a falling body, when he himself was killed. Because the chaplain's body is the first officially released from Ground Zero, his death certificate receives the number 1. Upon hearing of this, one firefighter said, "I just think God wanted somebody to lead the guys to heaven." Opposite: In a scene out of Dante, firefighters, hoping against hope, descend into the abyss.

A Brave One Departs

In awful conditions that make breathing an
endless effort, rescue workers on Sept. 12 bear
a stretcher carrying a flag-draped body, perhaps
a policeman. In all, 23 police officers perish in
the terrorist attack. Search and rescue efforts
are a 24-hour-a-day undertaking. Every person
involved wants more than anything to discover
a trapped survivor, or to unearth the body of
one of the many missing, so that frantic families
and friends can at least know the truth.

A City Transformed

In the aftermath of the attack, lower Manhattan ceases being a hub of commerce and becomes a neighborhood of makeshift triage centers and supply depots. A Burger King is commandeered by the police, while, on September 11 and for a few days thereafter, a Brooks Brothers store serves as a temporary morgue. Right: Policemen stand at an intersection near a clinic and a storage unit with body bags.

Ground Zero
The scale of the carnage wrought by the attack is immense. Rescue efforts are seriously hampered by the mountain of steel and stone that results from the destruction of two huge buildings. It is a frightful panorama, the physical manifestation of evil intent. Some estimates say it will take a year to tend to the area. Others maintain that it will take even longer.

Mario Tama/Getty

Two Faces of the Islamic World

The international reaction is swift, impassioned, sometimes frenzied. On the day itself, a Palestinian woman in Jerusalem's Old City celebrates an attack on what she considers an enemy nation. This image ignites a controversy when Palestinian officials, realizing the implications, try to suppress it, then claim that it was a setup. (The first effort fails; the allegation is proved untrue.) On Sept. 13 a woman holding a baby is led away for questioning by police in Hamburg, Germany, where cells of Islamic radicals were known to be operating. The roundup of suspects is global; in the U.S. hundreds of Islamists are detained.

Christina Caturano/AP

A Nation's Vigil

As it has only rarely in its history, the country pulls together, united citizens aching for their fallen brethren. Above, people gather at Boston's Church of Christ, Scientist to honor the dead. Candles are also on display at a shrine of remembrance in New York's Union Square (right), two miles from Ground Zero. Opposite: In Las Vegas, four-year-old Alana Milawski, supported by her daddy, Craig, waves one of the multitude of flags that are, suddenly, ubiquitous across the land.

Tom Stoddart/IPG/Matrix

Christopher Morris for Time/VII

Gary C. Knapp/AP (2)

In Time of War

As his shipmates raise the Stars and Stripes on the USS *Theodore Roosevelt,* a sailor in Norfolk, Va., shares an all-too-brief farewell with his wife. The military at home and abroad kicks into high gear immediately. Right, National Guardsmen, who soon become a familiar presence in New York and elsewhere, patrol lower Manhattan as Wall Street reopens.

Life After Death

Although the attack was one of the most alarming and worrying incidents in the history of the nation, Americans know that to hide under the bed is exactly what the terrorist aggressors want. The attack came on a Tuesday; basically, the country spent the rest of the week grieving, mulling over what had happened, getting a second wind. Then on the following Monday, it is time to get back on track. Baseball resumes, the stock market reopens. These kids in Hoboken, N.J., are fully involved in their soccer match, even as Ground Zero lies smoldering beyond.

Osama bin Laden

The moment the second plane hit the second tower in New York City, a name was mentioned. Was this, too, the work of a radical Islamist pledged to wage holy war against America?

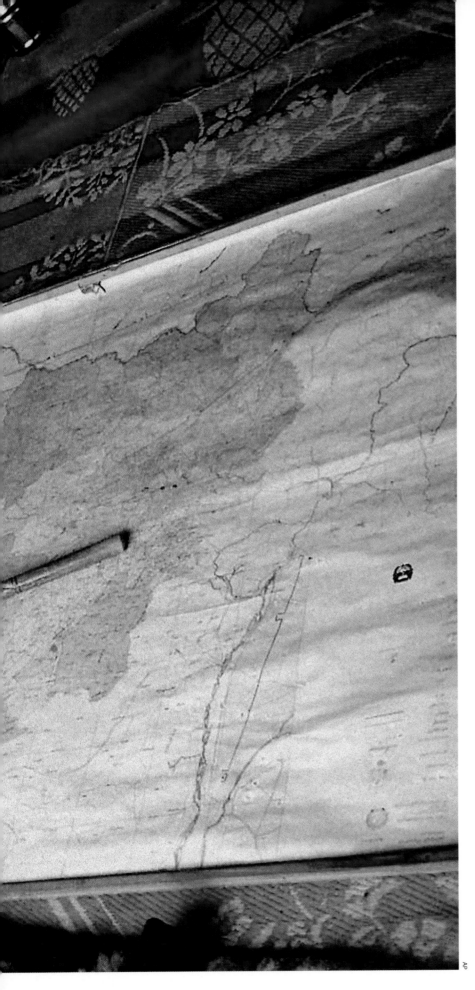

When the Taliban would not hand over bin Laden, putting in peril its government and thousand of lives, it was clear that Afghanistan's ruler was not some cleric in Kabul but the terrorist himself, calling his shots from a mountain lair.

Not since Hitler had America's rage and hatred been so intently focused on one man. Not since World War II had the nation been so united concerning the righteousness of its aim—to take the enemy, dead or alive.

For all that, on Sept. 10 there wasn't a citizen in 50 who could have told you much about Osama bin Laden. Big ratings for rebroadcasts of PBS biographies and big sales of scholarly books on Islam indicated just how scant the attention paid bin Laden had been, how little known the Muslim world. *He knew those men who bombed the Trade Center in 1993? He was behind the bombings of the African embassies and the U.S.S.* Cole? *They don't want our help in Saudi Arabia? What's this got to do with Israel? Who are these people? Who is this guy?*

He was, before he became The Prime Suspect (a.k.a. The Most Wanted Man in the World), a charismatic leader of a network of radical Islamist cells pledged to rid their holy land of infidels. Particularly galling to bin Laden and his al-Qaeda brethren was the presence of the U.S. military on Saudi soil during and since the Gulf War in 1990, as well as America's support of Israel, which continued to deny Palestinians a separate state. Washington was propping up dictatorships throughout the Middle East to protect its oil, ran this view, with willful disregard for a Muslim majority. Bin Laden declared a *jihad*—a holy war—against the U.S. from his Afghan redoubt and in 1998 made his intentions plain: "To kill Americans and their allies—civilians and military—is an individual duty for every Muslim who can do it."

Whether he had purchased nuclear bombs from Chechnya for $30 million in cash and two tons of heroin, as one report had it, or had built a huge arsenal of chemical and biological weaponry in the Afghan mountains, as others maintained, he had, without question, done something just as mind-boggling and terrifying: transformed himself from a benign, some say feckless, scion of a prominent

family into a leader for whom thousands if not millions would give their own lives to kill others. He was born in 1957 and was indulged as a child. When his father died in 1968, he inherited $80 million (his fortune as of September 11, which represented a part of al-Qaeda's financial bedrock, was variously estimated at $200 to $300 million). At King Abdul Aziz University, he became enthralled with a professor, Abdullah Azzam, a Palestinian who was a leader in the Muslim Brotherhood, an organization that spearheaded a 1970s resurgence in Middle Eastern religiosity and preached the notion of pan-Islamicism: a unification of the world's billion Muslims.

If Azzam was a crucial figure in bin Laden's evolution, the critical experience was his participation in the Afghan war against invading Soviets. Bin Laden enlisted in the fight in 1979 at age 22, seeing the non-Muslim intrusion on Islamic soil as an offense to God. Against heavy odds—and with covert U.S. aid—the fierce *mujaheddin* fought for more than a decade before forcing the Soviets to give up. When bin Laden saw the U.S. as a new godless intruder only a year later, he was convinced that his quest was blessed, and would prevail in any circumstance.

Clearly, for a long time before September 11 he was at war against the U.S., and even as his adopted country was overrun and the Taliban government brought down, he continued the fight. He has long felt that, in life or even in death, he continues the fight. There is evidence to support his belief, including a surge throughout the Islamic world of baby boys named Osama. If America's worst nightmare was realized on September 11, a horrific follow-up could be the martyrdom of Osama bin Laden: a hundred thousand others rising to take his place.

From high society to holy war. Below: Bin Laden père confers with King Faisal in 1969. Right: Osama (second from right) on holiday in Sweden with 21 of his 53 siblings in 1971. Above: On Oct. 7, praising the terrorists who attacked the U.S.

Fall

A Sign of the Times

Forever, people have looked to the heavens for signs,
omens of what the future may hold. No one knows
what this shooting star on Nov. 18 portended—better
days, many prayed—but we do know that it was part of
the Leonid shower, so named because it seems to
emanate from the constellation Leo. As many as 10
meteors a minute thrilled stargazers, who had been
waiting for this since the last big Leonid roared in 1966.
Causing the shower were particles, most smaller than a
grain of rice, which were shed by the comet Tempel-
Tuttle and ignited in Earth's atmosphere.

Photograph by William Coyle

The Burden of Decision

The President of the United States. It's a job that has often been called the loneliest in the world. When George W. Bush was elected, perhaps his wisest decision was to surround himself with sage, sober, seasoned veterans who could offer guidance during the incessant barrage of dilemmas that a Chief Executive must daily face. The past year provided some of the steepest, most treacherous hurdles in decades. Certainly the President seeks counsel on all matters, but when all is said and done, the man in charge must say yea or nay, for the buck truly does stop there. When Bush was elected, many wondered if he was up to the job. In 2001, most doubters were converted. Here, the President collected himself in the Speaker's Ceremonial Room of the Capitol before addressing a joint session of Congress.

Photograph by P.F. Bentley

> ❝ He isn't pushing too hard, but he's trying to keep things on the go . . . He is under control. ❞
>
> —**Edith Williams,** a retired fast-food worker in Richmond, and a Democrat

Oct. 7 Speaking on television about a half hour after explosions were reported in Kabul, President Bush says, "On my orders, the United States has begun strikes." **The military action,** involving cruise missiles, bombers and submarines, is carried out against a wide range of targets in Afghanistan.

Oct. 8 Radio talk show host Rush Limbaugh tells his 20 million listeners that **a rare inner ear disease** has left him nearly deaf. Doctors hope that an implant will enable the 50-year-old conservative commentator to continue broadcasting.

A Discouraging Word

It is one of the eeriest, grisliest words in the English language. Part of its impact lies in the fact that it isn't a word one hears very often. It is mostly reserved for horror stories from remote places; it's something perhaps best suited for the name of a too-loud rock band. But in the New Normal of life in the United States, all that has changed. "Anthrax" is a word we now read without pausing, hear on TV every day, utter to our friends in the most casual conversation. We know about its different forms, its different treatments. We now possess this word, and it, along with others like "smallpox" and "sarin," scares us. At right, a hazardous-materials worker in Fort Lauderdale donned his gear after anthrax was found near his community.

Photograph by Joe Raedle Getty

Oct. 11 The FBI issues a **security alert** that more terrorist attacks could be launched in the U.S. during the next several days. People are told to take the warning seriously while continuing to carry on normal lives. Two weeks later, Attorney General Ashcroft issues another alert, based on "credible information." The warnings draw criticism for alarming an already jittery nation without offering any specific guidance.

Oct. 12 The U.N. and its Secretary General, Kofi Annan, 63, are awarded the Nobel Peace Prize. Annan learns the news at five a.m. "It was **a wonderful way to wake up.** Given the sort of business we are in, usually when you get a call that early in the morning, it's something disastrous."

Oct. 20 **Rock icons** gather in Madison Square Garden to raise money for the victims of September 11. The show features Paul McCartney and Mick Jagger, but the real stars are 6,000 firefighters, police officers and rescue workers in attendance. Shows are also held in D.C. and Nashville.

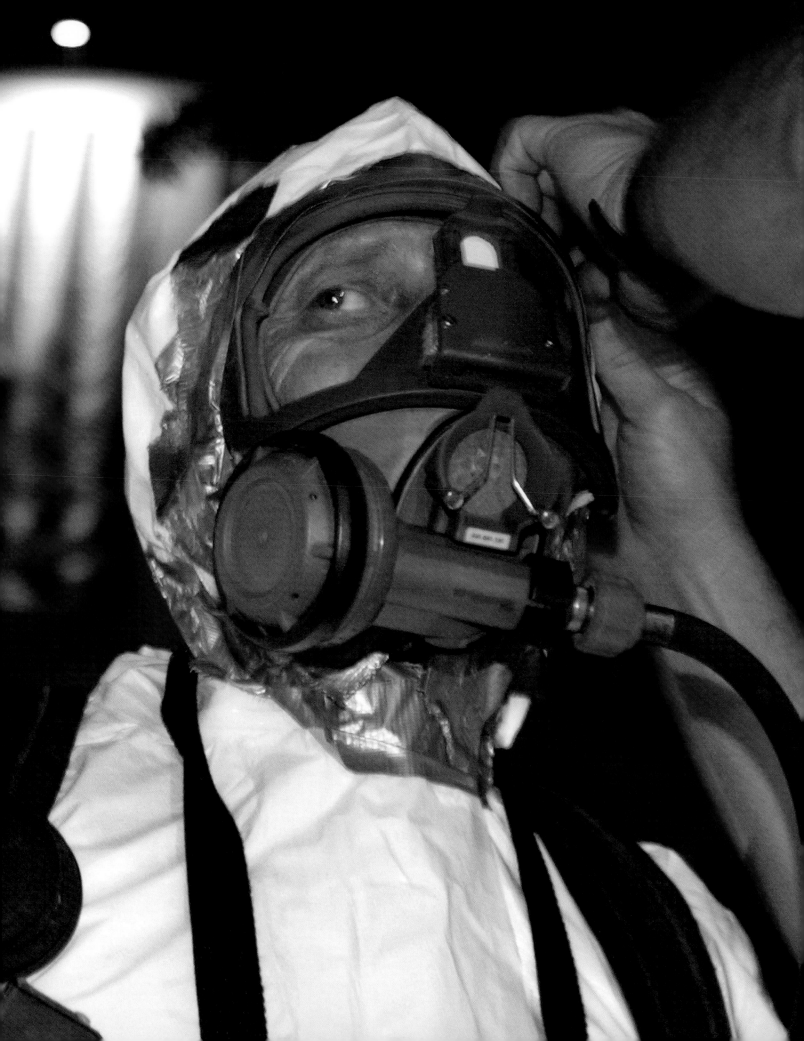

One Giant's Giant Step

With this graceful, mighty stroke, San Francisco's Barry Bonds thrilled the home crowd with his 73rd homer of the season, three taters more than Mark McGwire's record of 70 set in 1998. That year, McGwire and Sammy Sosa captivated the nation with a sizzling duel in which Roger Maris's 61 was left in the dust. In 2001, Bonds never quite aroused the same interest. Some critics groused that he was selfish; his fans called him misunderstood. But by any measure, Bonds had an astonishing 2001, and won an unprecedented fourth Most Valuable Player award.

Photograph by Heinz Kluetmeier and V.J. Lovero Sports Illustrated

❝ We have never seen a season like this in our lifetime, and we probably never will again. ❞

—**Ned Colletti,** Giants' assistant general manager, on Bonds's record-setting year

Nov. 1 California Governor Gray Davis says he has received "credible evidence" that **major bridges** in the state may be targets for terrorist attacks. National Guardsmen are called to tighten security on the spans.

Nov. 4 In the seventh game of the **World Series,** the Arizona Diamondbacks come from behind in the bottom of the ninth to stun the New York Yankees 3–2. Arizona pitchers Curt Schilling and Randy Johnson are voted co-MVPs.

Nov. 6 **Eighteen-year-old** Jeffrey Dunkel is elected mayor of Mount Carbon, Pa. Dunkel, who became interested in politics in high school, will be paid $50 a month to govern the town and its 100 residents.

Rarin' to Go

More than 15 months after a fiery crash that killed 113 people, the Concorde returned to its rarefied airspace on Nov. 7. Actually, three flights signaled the reappearance of the supersonic transport. An Air France plane carrying the company chairman and the French transport minister landed in New York at 8:30 a.m., and a British Airways SST bearing rock star Sting ("flying at twice the speed of sound gives you a buzz") touched down a little later. Mayor Giuliani welcomed the passengers and suggested they "spend a lot of money while you're here." The third flight brought America's newest best friend, British Prime Minister Tony Blair, to Washington for dinner with President Bush. At left, a Concorde gets spruced up at London's Heathrow Airport.

Photograph News Cast

Nov. 7 Lingling pummels the Philippines for two days, killing some 350 and leaving more than 200 missing. The name for the **vicious storm** is taken from a Chinese pet name for a young girl.

Nov. 11 **Mark McGwire,** 38, the first major leaguer to hit 70 home runs in one season, announces his retirement. The St. Louis Cardinals first baseman has been plagued by a knee problem for the past two years.

Nov. 13 After five weeks of war, Taliban troops **withdraw from Kabul.** The Islamic fundamentalist group has lost control of nearly half of Afghanistan as the hunt for Osama bin Laden intensifies.

Nov. 14 Eight aid workers, including two Americans, are rescued by anti-Taliban fighters and taken to Pakistan by U.S. military helicopters. The workers had been detained for more than three months on charges that they were **preaching Christianity to Muslims.**

All Too Familiar

On Nov. 12, American Airlines Flight 587, with 260 people on board, crashed in Belle Harbor, N.Y., three minutes after taking off. The Airbus 300, en route from John F. Kennedy International Airport to the Dominican Republic, went down in this residential neighborhood five miles from the airstrip. New York airports, bridges and tunnels were abruptly shut down, and TV networks were flooded with coverage. Many Americans, uncomfortably aware that the terrorist threat is ever present, worried that this might be part of a well-coordinated attack, and fear was in the air. An extremely thorough investigation, however, concluded that there had been no sabotage involved in the tragedy.

Photograph by Kristen Ashburn Contact

❝ I heard the engines very loud. They were loud and low, and because of what happened September 11, it gave me a chill. ❞

—**Phyllis Paul,** who lives near the crash site

Nov. 15 Philip Morris says it will change its name to Altria Group, drawing from the Latin *altus* ("high") to suggest high performance. **"Call for Altria"** doesn't quite have the ring of "Call for Philip Morrrissss," first enunciated by "Johnny" in radio ads in 1934.

Nov. 16 *Harry Potter and the Sorcerer's Stone,* the eagerly anticipated film version of J.K. Rowling's zillion-seller, debuts in the U.S. Critics are lukewarm but **kids love the movie,** which grosses $90.3 million, the biggest weekend opening ever.

All Is Bright

Holiday crowds gathered on New York City's Broad Street as the New York Stock Exchange tree was lighted in a ceremony honoring the firefighters, NYPD and Port Authority police officers and Emergency Medical Service Workers lost in the September 11 attack. The event carried particular significance, as the Exchange, like the World Trade Center, symbolizes American prosperity, even the very way of life that so infuriates and frustrates many of its foes. Attending the ceremony were Mayor Giuliani, Police Commissioner Bernard Kerik, Fire Chief Daniel Nigro and many children of the heroes who gave their lives on that infamous date.

Photograph by Andrew Savulich

Daily News

Nov. 21 Ottilie W. Lundgren of Oxford, Conn., becomes **the fifth victim of inhaled anthrax.** Five days after being admitted to the hospital, the 94-year-old woman dies from the same strain that was found in contaminated letters sent to government officials and the news media. Investigators are baffled by how the relatively inactive woman could have contracted the disease.

Nov. 25 Advanced Cell Technology, a small biotechnology company, announces it has **cloned** the first human embryos. Although experts call the experiment a failure because the embryos all died, the firm cites "the first proof that reprogrammed human cells can supply tissue for transplantation." President Bush calls for a ban on the use of embryos in cloning.

Dec. 3 Dean Kamen unveils his Segway Human Transporter, a one-person scooter that may or may not **revolutionize human mobility.** The self-balancing, battery-powered device, formerly code-named "Ginger," has a top speed of 17 mph.

In mid-November, Northern Alliance forces watch from a hillside as U.S. air strikes hit a Taliban position in Kunduz province. Meanwhile, in Chaman, Pakistan, an Afghan refugee girl exults after spotting an American fighter plane zooming overhead on another mission.

It is not a nation in the sense that Americans think of a nation. Throughout history, Afghanistan has continuously been reshaped, often by forces well beyond its fluctuating borders, and is today home to various peoples who despise one another to a degree that makes nationhood an absurd notion. Words that are used to describe factions and factors at work in Afghanistan—*tribal, feudal, warlord*—seem archaic to the modern ear. It's as if we are hearing stories of ancient Attilas and Genghises, or perhaps we're playing one of those fantastic computer games with crusaders storming the gates and horsemen chasing down the fleeing hordes.

But Afghanistan is no fantasy. In a land of surpassing natural beauty, many of the world's poorest, most beleaguered people now peer out from the rubble of the Taliban's reign and ask with trep-

FOCUS ON Afghanistan

In this complicated land, liberation does not necessarily mean freedom. A country plagued by eternal conflicts now asks an eternal question: What comes next?

In photographs emblematic of this war's brutality and of the hatred existing between Afghan tribes, a wounded Taliban soldier is dragged to his feet by Northern Alliance forces. He pleads for his life, then is beaten, executed and degraded. Above: The search for bin Laden means hunting in caves.

idation and fear, What could possibly be next? In their experience, they find no reason for optimism.

The Afghan situation is so extraordinarily complex that it renders impossible any effort at short summary. Nevertheless, some things can quickly be comprehended. Forces that shape the region include cultural and tribal loyalties (and schisms); religious affiliations (and varying degrees of fundamentalism); and terrorism. All these things overflow the country's boundaries as drawn on the map. Osama bin Laden's al-Qaeda outfit, if based in the mountains of Afghanistan, had—and has—global outposts, along with an inspirational reach that extends throughout the Islamic world, population 1 billion. No matter what U.S. and Northern Alliance troops achieve in Asia, the war against terrorism continues. So do tribal conflicts within Afghanistan. As its name implies, the Northern Alliance comprises

groups that, in the not distant past, were unaffili-ated on good days, rivals on bad ones. In pushing south with U.S. support they overran the territory of the Pashtun, the largest ethnicity in Afghanistan and the one that has, for centuries, regarded itself as the natural ruling body of the country. There are perhaps 20 million Pashtun living in a territory cre-ated by the British more than a century ago. This land, sometimes called Pashtunistan, is half in Afghanistan and half in Pakistan, and includes the city of Kabul. The Pashtun were allied with the Tal-iban, and it might be supposed that their influence will diminish in the new Afghanistan, but Pashtun

leaders do not view the situation this way.

And whither the Taliban? The group of hard-line Islamist leaders, persecutors of their country's cit-izenry and willing hosts to al-Qaeda, have paid a severe price for refusing to give up bin Laden. But it would be very wishful thinking to argue that a fundamentalist Muslim influence—which at the far end of the scale still presses a holy war against the U.S.—has been vanquished in Afghanistan.

We understand Afghanistan better than we did yesterday, surely, but still we do not understand Afghanistan. It changes daily, it will change tomor-row. Will it be for the better?

Anthony Suau for TIME

Derek Hudson/Matrix

Damir Sagolj/Getty Reuters

Shackles off and veils lifted, Afghans rush to the future. For five years, girls could not be schooled except in Taliban-free provinces held by the Northern Alliance. For five years, Afghans could see no movies. For five years, men had to go bearded. Today, razors are sharp, turnstiles are turning, and girls are learning.

Rudy Giuliani

Once in a great while, the unthinkable becomes real, and in a blurred instant the need arises for someone to come to the fore. It is in that moment that the measure of a man is taken.

Doug Mills/AP

On his first trip to New York City after the terrorist attacks, President Bush consoles the mayor. With them is Governor George Pataki, who frequently shares the stage with Giuliani during the many press conferences that attend the tragedy; the two men seem unfettered by past differences. Opposite: A moment of silence at a Yankee Stadium service for the victims.

RUDY—it's a name engineered for tabloid headlines in a city whose daily pulse is best measured on a Richter-scale level. RUDY is about a man who lives in, and for, a solar public glare. RUDY arouses inflamed passions and connotes tough-noogie notions of right and wrong. RUDY is not for the faint of heart.

Right?

For better or worse, it certainly used to be. For six years of his tenure, it was right as rain. But two years ago, Hizzoner had to make some life-altering decisions. And then came September 11, 2001.

Born in 1944 to a working-class family in Brooklyn, Rudolph W. Giuliani graduated magna cum laude from NYU Law School. He quickly ascended the ranks of the Southern District of New York,

where he was appointed U.S. Attorney. Like a mongoose among cobras, Giuliani pursued and put away organized crime figures and drug dealers, etching a record of 4,152 convictions against only 25 losses. After losing the mayoral race by a whisker in 1989, Giuliani, campaigning on crime and quality of life, became the mayor of New York in 1993.

It is a preposterous assignment, traditionally second only to President as the toughest job in the land. One is beset at every turn by savage infighting and political potholes nearly as big as those on Bruckner Boulevard. Yet Giuliani came through on his campaign vow. Crime was halved, and the FBI rated the streets of New York the safest of any large city in the country for five straight years. Giuliani also cut the welfare rolls in half, as 640,000 people learned to provide for themselves.

Timothy Fadek/Gamma

Early on the morning of Sept. 12, the mayor lowers his dust mask while visiting Ground Zero. A month later, he is joined at the site by Britain's Prince Andrew and Police Commissioner Bernard Kerik.

It was a remarkable turnaround, but RUDY didn't lack for critics. Many in the black community felt profoundly neglected, and the public school system was a disgrace. Public housing was clearly inadequate. On top of it all, for many New Yorkers, the man's very style rankled: cold, cunning, take no prisoners, ask questions later.

Still and all, the populace was sufficiently taken with Giuliani's record that he stood an excellent chance in 2000 to win election to the U.S. Senate. The media was gaga over the prospect of RUDY taking on HILLARY in a campaign that would set a new standard for chain-saw invective. Then fate stepped in. In April 2000 the mayor revealed that he had early-stage prostate cancer, and a few weeks later, saying that he wanted to "put my health first," he dropped out of the race. Treatment for the cancer went perfectly, but the decision stood, and Giuliani would remain a mayor until term limits ended his stay at City Hall on the last day of 2001.

Even as the mayor's illness was a large story, another serious drama began playing itself out in the press. In May 2000, Giuliani announced at a daily news briefing that he was seeking a separation agreement from his wife, the actress Donna Hanover. The couple, who married in 1983 and had

Giuliani escorts Judy Nathan to a tribute in his honor. Right: The mayor attends a service at St. Patrick's Cathedral for firefighter Christian Regenhard, an ex-Marine and the son of a retired police officer. Bottom: Yankees manager Joe Torre hugs Giuliani before a game. Unlike other New York pols, he had eyes for only one team.

two kids, shared an often volatile relationship and hadn't been seen together much for a few years. In fact, Giuliani was frequently in the company of Judith Nathan, director of a New York–based philanthropy, of whom he said, "We're very good friends." The public, lawyer-fueled vitriol that ensued between the estranged couple was not at all pretty, and a perfect, bizarre tabloid note was sounded when Hanover signed on to appear in the off-Broadway feminist play *The Vagina Monologues*.

Giuliani emerged from the testing ground of 2000 a changed man. Struggling publicly with the difficulties that confront a cancer victim, he seemed perceptibly to soften. "I think I understand myself a lot better," he said, as he dedicated the duration of his term to fighting racial inequality in the city.

His latter days in office were playing out in comparative tranquillity when the terrorist attack exploded at 8:47 a.m. on September 11, 2001. Minutes later, Giuliani was racing downtown to the Trade Center. He first went to a fire command post that would later be crushed. Then he and his aides went a block away to set up a communications center, but debris forced them, dust-covered and in harm's way, to relocate.

These were the first moments of an awesome display of steadying strength and innate leadership that inspired a community, and a nation. During a grinding ordeal that would test anyone, the mayor seemed always to be at the right place, to say the right thing. He helped keep the great city from panicking, from giving in to the terrorists. "That's just what they want," he would say, rallying New Yorkers to go out to restaurants and shops, imploring tourists to come to the city as a way of contributing to the huge relief effort. There was never a false note as he handled the dreadful responsibility of consoling thousands of mourners. His performance was stunning, and even his most severe critics conceded that this man had done what few others could have in that crisis: lead with vigor, dignity and humanity. In the terrible alembic of terrorism and war, RUDY had become Rudy.

LIFE Remembers

In this most difficult of years, others, too, were lost: giants of the screen who made us laugh and cry, great writers who fired our imaginations, leaders who inspired us, musicians who stirred us. By year's end, the Fab Four numbered only two.

George Harrison

The older lads took him into the band when he was just 14 years old because he knew a lot of chords. Indeed. In just a few years he would burst into solar-system-size fame as the lead guitarist for the biggest band that ever played popular music: the Beatles. And in the midst of some formidable competition from his supremely talented mates, he more than held his own. His guitar work helped shape their fab sound, he was a decent singer and fine harmonizer, and he wrote some terrific songs, by turns jaunty and introspective. In the latter vein, he was an important influence on the direction of the band (and by extension, legions of young people) through his interest in Eastern religion and music. This spiritual aspect enticed him to numerous charitable acts, including 1971's concert for Bangladesh relief, the first giant rock charity effort, which was echoed in 2001 by Paul McCartney's concert—also held at Madison Square Garden—for the victims of September 11. Under his own name, Harrison made many fine recordings, particularly his masterwork collection, *All Things Must Pass*. The quiet Beatle died of cancer at 58.

Max Scheler/K & K/Star File

Everett Collection

Katharine Graham

She was born in 1917 into such a wealthy, pampered life that as a college student she had to be gently reminded that clothes need laundering. Graham lacked confidence and direction until 1963 when she took over her father's *Washington Post* after her dashing husband, who had been running the paper, killed himself. Partnering with editor Ben Bradlee, she bravely guided the once banal *Post* through the Pentagon Papers and Watergate, two of journalism's most celebrated episodes. One of the nation's foremost business leaders, she was also the queen bee of D.C. society. Said Bradlee: "Kay was a spectacular dame."

Jack Lemmon

Before each scene, he murmured to himself, "Magic time." The son of a doughnut company exec, Lemmon was born in an elevator in 1925, studied at Harvard and served as an ensign in the Navy. With his eager face and sad eyes he was for five decades the American Everyman—"I'm attracted primarily to contemporary characters. I understand them and their frustrations." He showed a genius early on for light comedy, in the '50s flicks *Mister Roberts* and *Some Like It Hot*, but a palpable sincerity also produced scalding dramatic performances (*Missing, Glengarry Glen Ross*). In his career, there were two great comrades. Actor Walter Matthau's weariness was the perfect foil for Lemmon's untamed energy, while Lemmon's innocence was the perfect ingredient in the cynical comedies of director Billy Wilder, who once said, "Happiness is working with Jack Lemmon."

Perry Como

With his comforting cardigan and mellow baritone, he put the easy in easy listening. Born the seventh son of a seventh son in Canonsburg, Pa., in 1912, Como had his own barbershop by the age of 14, but with "more than a few misgivings," he yielded to the performing urge in 1933. Good decision. He had 50 Top 10 records ("Prisoner of Love," "Catch a Falling Star") and sold 100 million albums, starred in radio and movies, and was a fixture in the TV variety shows he helped pioneer. A pipeline to the living room, television was the ideal medium for one whom Bing Crosby dubbed "the man who invented casual."

Imogene Coca

From 1950 to 1954, this wide-eyed, rubber-limbed gamine was a 24-karat-pure comedienne in the Golden Age of Television, blending blissfully with Sid Caesar on the classic *Your Show of Shows*. Though shy offstage, showbiz was a natural for Coca, who was born in 1908 to an orchestra conductor and an actress-dancer. After *Show* she worked steadily, but always in lesser vehicles.

Isaac Stern

The first American-trained violinist to achieve world-class status, he was born in the Ukraine in 1920, then taken by his parents as an infant to San Francisco. His brilliant technique and warm tone informed his emotional interpretation of classical music from the Baroque to 20th century masters. Stern's other grand passion was Carnegie Hall, which he helped save from demolition in 1960 by fronting a campaign of artists and civic leaders. "It's not only a building," said Stern. "It's an idea. It's a necessary mythology about music."

Chet Atkins

They called him Mr. Guitar, for his deft picking as a soloist and as a studio cat who sat in with everyone from Elvis and the Everlys to Waylon and Willie. But he also struck gold as a record producer and executive when he refined the twang of hillbilly music with strings and background vocals, creating the sophisticated-yet-casual Nashville Sound that lifted country into the big-market world it inhabits today. The pride of Luttrell, Tenn., was 77.

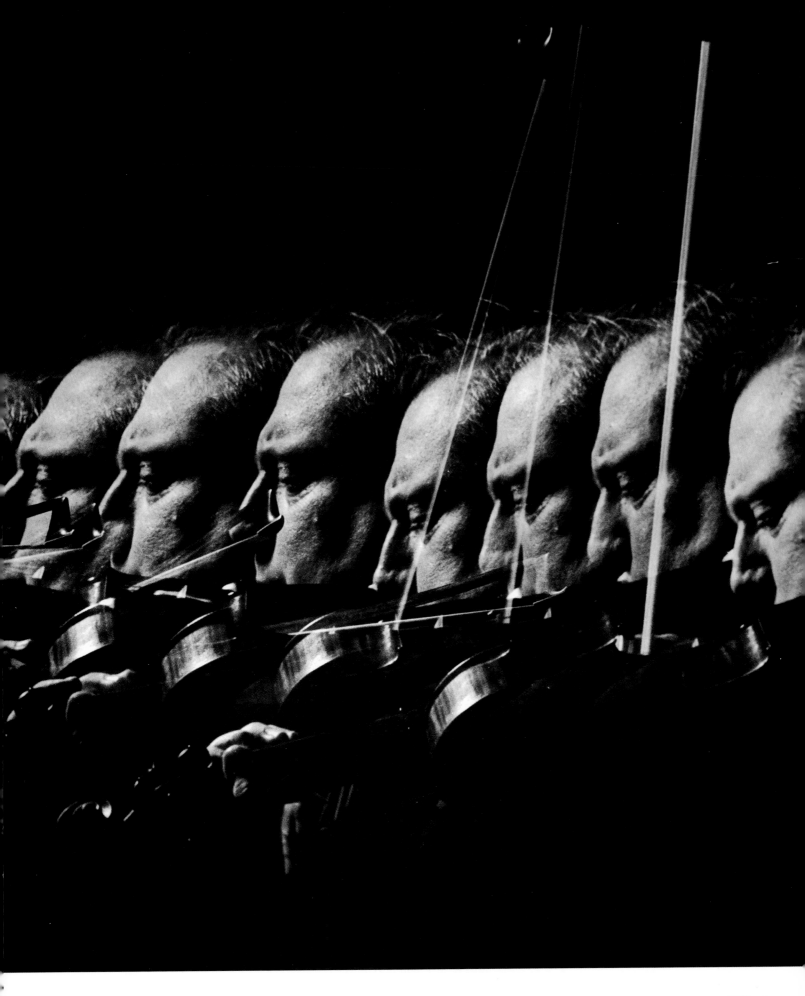

John Phillips

Born in Parris Island, S.C., to a career military family, he withdrew from Annapolis and set sail for Greenwich Village, where he kicked around the coffeehouse circuit. In 1964 he gathered Cass Elliott, Denny Doherty and wife Michelle to form the seminal folk-rock group the Mamas and the Papas. Drawing on Phillips's plaintive writing and potent arranging, they crafted such timeless hits as "California Dreamin'" and "Monday, Monday," all the while mixing drugs with internecine romance. Papa John died at 65, survived by performing daughters Mackenzie, Chynna and Bijou.

Jonathan Mannion

Aaliyah

This R&B singer joined an all-too-long line of young pop-star tragedies when she died at age 22 in a small-plane crash. Born Aaliyah Dana Haughton in Brooklyn, she was raised in Detroit, where she began singing. At age 11 her aunt Gladys Knight invited her to perform in Las Vegas. Three years later, Aaliyah recorded the first of three smash albums, and in 2000 appeared in her first movie, *Romeo Must Die*. Rapper DMX was also in that film, and he called Aaliyah "talented, classy, warm, beautiful . . . with enough energy to put anyone on a cloud."

Mimi Fariña

She began performing lyrical folk music with her husband, singer-writer Richard Fariña, in 1964, two years before he died in a motorcycle crash on her birthday. Then, after some false starts, she found her lovely soprano voice again. In 1974 she formed Bread and Roses, which brings live music to the institutionalized. Fariña, Joan Baez's younger sister, died after a long struggle with cancer at 56.

Michael Ochs Archive

Roger Ressmeyer

John Lee Hooker

One of 11 children, he was born in 1917 in the Mississippi Delta to a Baptist minister and sharecropper. He became one of the greats of post-WWII blues, the father of the boogie, a hypnotic, foot-slammin', one-note blues that Hooker wrought to perfection with his open-tuned guitar and brooding, unyielding baritone. Hooker's legacy lives in 100 albums, and his influence on British and American rock 'n' rollers cannot be overstated.

Joe Henderson

One of the legendary tenor saxmen and composers, this native Ohioan blew onto the New York jazz scene in 1962, a genius who could embroider a melody or turn up the heat with fiery licks. He teamed early with the likes of Horace Silver and Herbie Hancock, then on his own he made a slew of first-rate albums, from the trio setting of *The State of the Tenor* to *The Joe Henderson Big Band*. A battle with emphysema finally claimed the Phantom at age 64.

Susannah McCorkle

A rare blend of wit, brains and great chops, this smoky-voiced singer thrived in the realm of 20th century songwriters like Gershwin, Porter and Jobim. Her albums and cabaret shows were delightful essays spun from her repertory of more than 3,000 songs. She was dedicated, as well, to bringing music into schools. Unfortunately, she suffered from severe bouts of depression, and at age 55 she leapt to her death from her Manhattan apartment.

Horst Tappe

Anthony Quinn

"I was never accepted as an American. The blond boys were the heroes. So I played the villains." It is true that in the litany of exotics played by Quinn in some 150 roles—Filipino, Libyan, Chinese, Basque, Eskimo et al.—he rarely got the girl. He was, however, a bastion of fiery strength and moral persuasiveness. The man himself was of Mexican-Irish stock, and had 13 children by five women. Eyebrows were raised five years before his death at age 86 when it was revealed that he had yet another son on the way. He copped Supporting Oscars for *Viva Zapata!* and *Lust for Life* (in which he was onscreen only eight minutes) but missed with his immortal *Zorba the Greek*.

Dale Evans

Born in 1912, life was rocky at the start for Evans, who entered school late, eloped at 14, had a baby and was divorced by 16. But in 1944 the singer-actress costarred with the "King of the Cowboys," Roy Rogers, and the "Queen of the West" began her reign. They married three years later, and in 27 films and a classic TV show, she and Rogers, along with their ponies Buttermilk and Trigger, formed a posse of modest, decent, straight-shootin' folks. She endured several tragedies with her children, prompting her to write 20 inspirational books. In the words of their theme song, which she penned, Happy trails to you, Dale Evans.

Carroll O'Connor

Perhaps more than any other character in the history of television, Archie Bunker became a household name, and a volatile one. Carroll O'Connor, who died at 76, inhabited that role brilliantly. To many, Bunker was a benighted bigot with a caveman mentality, a buffoon living in a world of fear and antagonism. To others he was a hero, a regular guy who, at last, laid it on the line. In any case, in the '70s the *All in the Family* character erased the sitcom image of the infallible, reassuring American dad. As the show's creator, Norman Lear, said, "He is etched permanently in our memories." O'Connor's later years were poisoned when his adopted son, Hugh, killed himself in a drug-related suicide in 1995.

Loomis Dean

Robert W. Kelley

Mike Mansfield

During his 34 years in Congress, 16 of them as Senate majority leader, this laconic but resolute Democrat was vital in crafting legislation in the 1960s and '70s on civil rights and foreign affairs. Born in New York City's Greenwich Village in 1903, he was sent to Montana at age three after his Irish-immigrant mother died. When he lied about his age (14) to enter the Navy, he began a lifetime of service that culminated with 11 years as ambassador to Japan. Senate colleague Hugh Scott called him "the most decent man I've ever met in public life."

Nguyen Van Thieu

The youngest child of a simple rice farmer, he became president of South Vietnam in 1967. At first considered a stable, unifying force, he became extremely rigid and excessively cautious, despite enormous financial and military aid from the U.S. Two years after the 1973 American withdrawal, Thieu was routed by a North Vietnamese offensive and forced to flee Saigon. He lived in London and later Boston until his death at 76.

H. Tyler

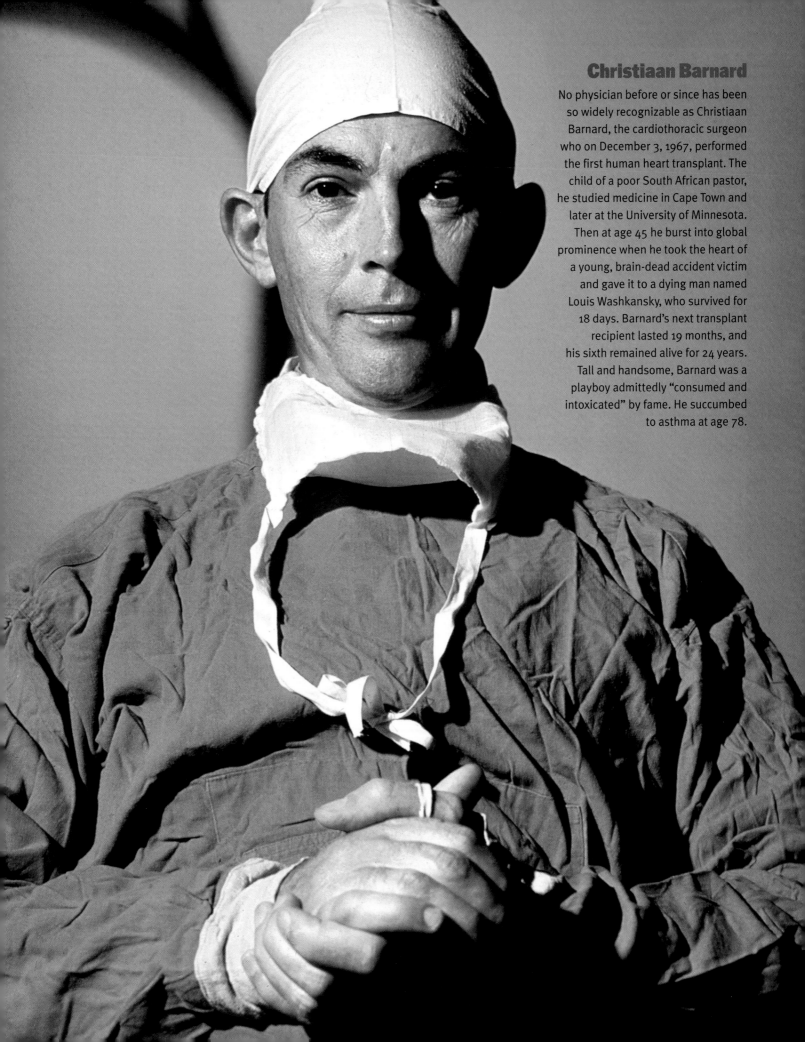

Christiaan Barnard

No physician before or since has been so widely recognizable as Christiaan Barnard, the cardiothoracic surgeon who on December 3, 1967, performed the first human heart transplant. The child of a poor South African pastor, he studied medicine in Cape Town and later at the University of Minnesota. Then at age 45 he burst into global prominence when he took the heart of a young, brain-dead accident victim and gave it to a dying man named Louis Washkansky, who survived for 18 days. Barnard's next transplant recipient lasted 19 months, and his sixth remained alive for 24 years. Tall and handsome, Barnard was a playboy admittedly "consumed and intoxicated" by fame. He succumbed to asthma at age 78.

Herblock

He was a gentle fellow, born Herbert Lawrence Block in Chicago in 1909, but as the cartoonist Herblock he was a devastating foe of conniving public figures. For seven decades, mostly with *The Washington Post,* he skewered politicians the world over, most memorably Richard Nixon and Senator Joseph McCarthy, both of whom he depicted as rising up from the sewer. His work earned him three Pulitzer Prizes and a share of a fourth.

Hank Ketcham

In 1950, Ketcham was a freelance cartoonist when his wife said that their son, Dennis, was "a menace." By the next year, a nation bursting with baby boomers became entranced with Dennis the Menace, a five-year-old towheaded tornado who terrorized grumpy Mr. Wilson and prissy nemesis Margaret. Ketcham used comedy writers for the strip, which ran in 1,000 newspapers and 48 countries and inspired a TV show and movie, but drew it himself until 1994. After a tour of duty in Vietnam, the real-life Dennis suffered post-traumatic stress disorder and lost touch with his father, who died at 81.

Ken Kesey

A self-styled counterculture writer and activist, he was a longtime champion of hallucinogens and used them while writing his two big novels, *One Flew Over the Cuckoo's Nest* and *Sometimes a Great Notion*. In 1964 he traveled from California to New York and back in a psychedelic bus (Kesey, left, with fellow tripper Neal Cassady) carrying a zany group called the Merry Pranksters, who wanted to experience the American road while high on LSD. He died at 66 after liver cancer surgery.

Martha Holmes

Pauline Kael

She began reviewing movies in 1953, and over the next four decades, mostly at *The New Yorker,* became probably the most influential film critic in the world. Wickedly funny and always provocative, she drew on her considerable intellectualism to relate movies to a wide array of disciplines, along the way skewering highbrow criticism, most notably the auteur theory, which she reviled. She was 82.

Balthus

One of the most enigmatic figures of 20th century art, he was born Balthazar Klossowski de Rola in Paris in 1908. An associate of Rilke, Bonnard and Giacometti, Balthus was a precise draftsman whose figurative canvases (he also did stage designs) had no use for abstraction. His critics found them kitschy. He was best known for portraits and landscapes, along with erotic depictions of adolescent girls.

Jill Krementz

Anne Morrow Lindbergh

A painfully shy young woman, she married perhaps the most famous person in the world in 1929. As the wife of "Lucky Lindy," solo conqueror of the Atlantic, she became an expert aviator herself, often joining her husband on trailblazing flights. But the skies blackened in 1932 with the most publicized personal tragedy of the 20th century: The Lindbergh's kidnapped 20-month-old first child, Charles, was found dead in the woods near their New Jersey estate. Of the attendant media frenzy, she later said, "I felt like an escaped convict. This was not freedom." The couple fled to Europe for privacy, then returned during World War II to find their image tarnished by their isolationist views. Lindbergh wrote several books, notably 1955's best-seller, *Gift from the Sea*, a series of feminist reflections. She was 94.

Underwood and Underwood

Deborah Feingold/Corbis Outline

Eudora Welty

Born in Jackson, Miss., in 1909, this lyrical writer used myth and allusion to compress the soul of the Deep South until it became a magical diamond of universal truth. Dismissed early as a "regionalist," her sharp wit and keen ear for speech elevated her short stories to the level of comparison with Chekhov's. Welty could also expand to a novel, as with the 1973 Pulitzer winner *The Optimist's Daughter*.

Robert Ludlum

A powerful engine that spewed out international thrillers bearing three-word titles, Ludlum was in his forties when he published his first of 22 novels. He would sell more than 200 million books. His tales were overrun with italics and exclamation points, but they were fun. As one *Washington Post* reviewer said, "It's a lousy book. So I stayed up until three a.m. to finish it." The suspense master was 73.

The Victims of September 11

At year's end, many were still listed as missing. Yet it was clear that some 3,500 were killed in New York on the fateful day, with 157 dead on the two hijacked planes; at the Pentagon, 189 were dead or missing, with 64 killed on that airliner; and 44 perished in Pennsylvania when the fourth plane crashed. At the National City Christian Church in Washington, D.C., on Sept. 14, a mourner bade them rest in peace.